INTRODUCTION TO
Watercolour, gouache and tempera

INTRODUCTION TO
Watercolour, gouache and tempera

Ronald Pearsall

Brian Trodd Publishing House Limited

Previous page: Shady Pool by
J. S. Cotman

The Gleaning Field by Samuel
Palmer.

First published in 1990 by
Brian Trodd Publishing House Limited
27 Swinton Street, London WC1X 9NW

ISBN 1 85361 096 8

Printed in Portugal

CONTENTS

Introduction   11

What Are Watercolours?   12

What Materials Are Needed?   12

Is the Watercolour Wash the
   Very First Step to a Painting?   30

Drawing and Perspective   36

     Landscape and townscape   43

     Figure studies and portraits   65

     Still life   72

Gouache   78

Short Cuts   90

The White House by Thomas
Girtin.

Introduction

Painting in watercolours offers an immense scope for everybody. There is no end to the number of methods you can use, and watercolour can be used not only by itself but with pastels, coloured pencils, pen and ink, and acrylics – anything which is compatible with water.

You may wish to restrict yourself to what is known as the English method of watercolour painting, which means using the paints without the addition of white, as you use the white of the paper by allowing it to show through. Or you may wish to use not only thin washes but thick paint, and you have it in gouache. Gouache is well known to children in the form of powder paint, but refined it comes under a variety of names, such as designers' colours, poster paint, etc.

You work out the style which suits *you*. If you are good at drawing, you may like to create a picture meticulously and then colour it in. For added crispness, you may care to go round the shapes with a very fine pen. If you are no good at drawing, don't be alarmed. You can paint a perfectly good watercolour, without ever needing to touch a pencil, by relying on changes of colour and tone.

The accent of this book is on enjoyment. Nobody is paying you for painting a picture. But the satisfaction of creating something which only you can do can be unbelievable. Every person has the seeds of an artist in him or her. We just need encouraging!

WHAT ARE WATERCOLOURS?

Pigment mixed with a gum which acts as a binder; this binder is soluble in water. The traditional gum was gum arabic (which naturally came from Arabia) but it has been largely replaced by gum from a species of acacia tree grown in Africa. Gouache or opaque watercolour varies in quality from ordinary distemper to designers' colour.

Watercolour painting is older than oil painting, and was used by monks for illustrating manuscripts before they found that gouache, mixing their watercolour pigments with white, provided a better base for the inevitable gold embellishment. In the 17th century Dutch painters added a little colour to their drawings to liven them up; tinted drawings then became fashionable, the colours limited to blue, yellow, green, brown and rose madder. Among the first English artists to use the tinted drawing style was Francis Barlow (1626–1702). Watercolours were not regarded as at all important, but were records, notes for oil paintings, or sketches for engravings. Early papers were thin and fragile, and artists were obliged to scrape them to make them serviceable. Many artists made their own inks, sepia or black, and diluted them so that they could supplement pen-and-ink work with a thin ink wash.

Topographical artists commonly used a single wash, but the more adventurous found there were great possibilities in several washes, and different ways of applying paint, in dabs as used by David Cox or stippling where the paint is applied in the form of dots, as exploited by Birket Foster in innumerable village cottage scenes. Lifting the colour from the paper to expose highlights was done extensively by using rag, India-rubber, blotting paper, or dry bread. Francis Nicholson anticipated the use of masking fluid by applying a mixture of turpentine, beeswax and white, over which he painted his washes. When the wash had dried, he would lift his mixture with turpentine.

Shadows were put in with prussian blue and brown ink, and later by darker tones of the local colour. John Sell Cotman and Turner achieved their highlights by taking off the wet paint with the wooden end of the brush. This left a hard dark edge by creating a kind of canal at the edge of the highlight, an effect impossible to get with the brush and less brutal than lifting the colour off with a knife. John Varley's device was to paint upon thin paper laid on white card, and when he wanted a highlight he would scratch right through the paper so that the white of the card would show through.

Those watercolour artists who also did engravings found that they could duplicate drawings very well by taking blacklead impressions from an etched plate. It was very convenient for those who worked to a formula. Each watercolourist had his favourite colour scheme; John Cozens (1752–1799) used a basic palette of greys and blues with a very restricted use of brighter colours. John Webber (1750–1793) used blues, greys and light yellows.

Many 19th-century artists applied the paint to the paper without pencil drawings, using the splashes and blobs as a basis for a composition, others used rich watercolour to make a mosaic, and others returned to the tinted drawing format, with a difference. The works of Arthur Rackham and Edmund Dulac are tokens of what can be done in book illustration and are superb watercolour paintings in their own right. Watercolour lends itself equally to atmospheric suggestiveness or precision, and can do almost anything required.

WHAT MATERIALS ARE NEEDED?

Watercolours come in tubes or pans, sold in sets or separately. Artists' colours are a good deal more expensive than students' colours, which can be slightly grainy (though this can be an advantage as it provides interesting textures). Opaque watercolours, under whatever name, are sold in tubes, pans or jars; designers' colours are the best, though poster paint sold in jars is useful for covering large areas as it is cheaper. White gouache is sometimes known as process white and is sold in jars, and is extremely useful for eradicating mistakes on pen-and-ink work and pencil drawings. It can also be used to accompany ordinary transparent watercolour, either to provide highlights,

Watercolours provide a perfect medium for the artist to express himself by the quickness of technique and to capture the mood and atmosphere of his subject, as in this painting *Hurricane Bahamas* by Winslow Homer

or as a mix, when it is known as body colour. Watercolour in tubes is very concentrated, and a little goes a long way. For outdoor work a paint box with pans is the most convenient.

Mediums Normally the only medium needed is water, but gum arabic can be added, and so can megilp, which gives added brilliance and retards the drying.

Above: At first glance Alfred Jacob Miller's *Trappers Resting on the Trail* is of tightness and detail. Closer examination shows that it is just a collection of simple washes which make up the whole.

Right: The Needles by J. S. Cotman. A limited palette has produced this remarkable watercolour with only the boats in the foreground to give details.

Liquitex® Artist Water Colors
Tube Size ½" x 3¼", 6 per box

Color No.		Series 1841 Per Tube 6 tubes/box
110	ACRA® Crimson	●
112	ACRA® Red	●
114	ACRA® Violet	●
116	Alizarine Crimson	●
127	Burnt Siena	●
128	Burnt Umber	●
150	Cadmium Orange	●
152	Cadmium Red Light	●
154	Cadmium Red Medium	●
155	Cadmium Red Deep	●
160	Cadmium Yellow Light	●
161	Cadmium Yellow Med.	●
162	Cadmium Yellow Deep	●
164	Cerulean Blue	●
166	Chromium Oxide Green	●
170	Cobalt Blue	●
172	Cobalt Violet	●
186	Dioxazine Purple	●
190	Emerald Green	●
214	Green Earth	●
220	Hansa Yellow	●
224	Hooker's Green	●
225	Hooker's Green Light	●
240	Indian Red	●
244	Ivory Black	●
250	Lampblack	●
252	Lemon Yellow Hansa	●
258	Light Red Oxide	●
272	Manganese Blue	●
310	Payne's Gray	●
312	Permanent Green Light	●
316	Phthalocyanine Blue	●
317	Phthalocyanine Green	●
318	Prussian Blue	●
330	Raw Siena	●
331	Raw Umber	●
344	Rose Madder	●
360	Sepia Umber	●
380	Ultramarine Blue	●
388	Ultramarine Violet	●
390	Van Dyke Brown Umber	●
398	Viridian	●
413	Yellow Ochre	●
430	Zinc (Chinese) White	●

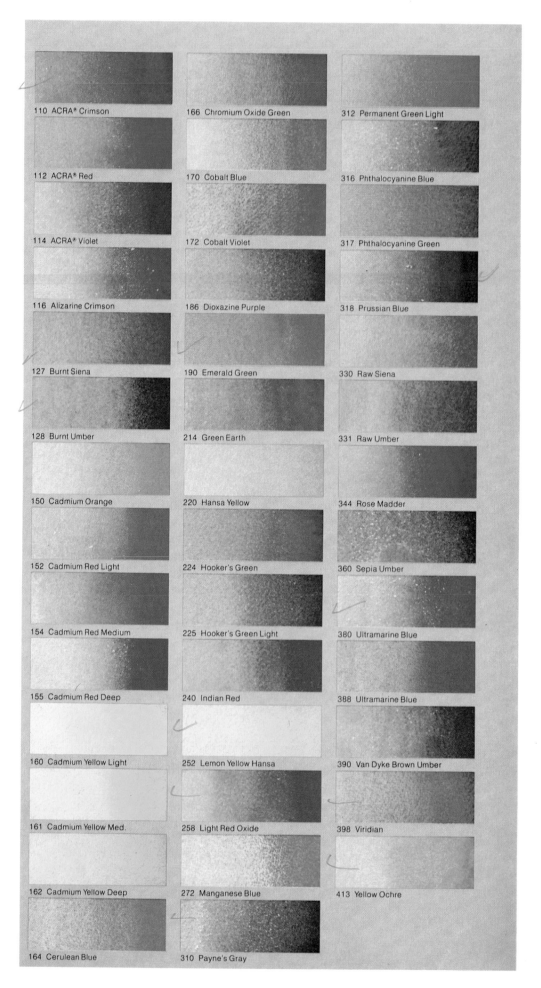

110 ACRA® Crimson   166 Chromium Oxide Green   312 Permanent Green Light

112 ACRA® Red   170 Cobalt Blue   316 Phthalocyanine Blue

114 ACRA® Violet   172 Cobalt Violet   317 Phthalocyanine Green

116 Alizarine Crimson   186 Dioxazine Purple   318 Prussian Blue

127 Burnt Siena   190 Emerald Green   330 Raw Siena

128 Burnt Umber   214 Green Earth   331 Raw Umber

150 Cadmium Orange   220 Hansa Yellow   344 Rose Madder

152 Cadmium Red Light   224 Hooker's Green   360 Sepia Umber

154 Cadmium Red Medium   225 Hooker's Green Light   380 Ultramarine Blue

155 Cadmium Red Deep   240 Indian Red   388 Ultramarine Blue

160 Cadmium Yellow Light   252 Lemon Yellow Hansa   390 Van Dyke Brown Umber

161 Cadmium Yellow Med.   258 Light Red Oxide   398 Viridian

162 Cadmium Yellow Deep   272 Manganese Blue   413 Yellow Ochre

164 Cerulean Blue   310 Payne's Gray

Brushes To an artist a brush is as important as a violin to a violinist or a chisel to a carpenter, and this applies just as much when you are a beginner. A great range of sizes and shapes is available and care is required when making your choice. Sable brushes are regarded as the best for watercolours, so it is wise to invest in these even if they cost more at the outset. If treated well they will last for several years. Cheap brushes (ox hair, camel hair, etc.) are a false economy, though some nylon ones may be satisfactory for some purposes. Do not stint on the number of brushes in your watercolour kit, and get a good range from size 00 upwards, including pointed brushes, flat square brushes, and the long thin brushes known as 'liners' (used for drawing lines but ideal for any kind of detailed work). 'Fan' brushes are also useful and excellent for blending in washes. To test a pointed brush wet it, shake out the excess water, and roll it on the palm of the hand to form a point. If the point is thin and weak, reject it; if there is too much 'belly' the brush may hold too much water and be difficult to handle. If any hairs come out during this test, the brush is past redemption. Oil-painting brushes can also be useful and so can old toothbrushes (which give a good 'splatter' effect) and shaving brushes, for texture and for loading a paper with water.

Some professional artists use soft Chinese and Japanese brushes which often have cane handles. These were intended for calligraphy and they are used as writing instruments in their countries of origin and not for washes.

When brushes have been used they should be washed in water and left to dry at room temperature, with hairs uppermost, in a jar or other container, and although during a painting session brushes are frequently and unconsciously dropped hairs – down in the water container this is not to be recommended for any length of time. Some colours clean off the brush easier than others; greens always seem to lodge in the hairs and bristles.

For artists who like to do outdoor work special containers are available so that they can carry their brushes around without damaging them; but even better is to fix the brush, with an elastic band, to a narrow piece of card which is slightly taller than the brush. Then use another piece of card, the same size, as a cover. Many small sable brushes when sold have little plastic covers over the hairs, and these could be well worth keeping for outdoor excursions.

Palettes Paint boxes usually have three depressions in the lid to serve as a palette, but these are not very practical, and divided dishes are better. As you will not be standing up to paint with watercolour (and therefore you will not need an easel) the dish for your paint should be by your hand rather than in it. Tin and plastic containers divided into up to eight sections are excellent, but ordinary household saucers can be used, as well as dinner plates.

Far left: Watercolour chart showing the large variety available.

Below: A selection of watercolour materials, a few of the vast range available.

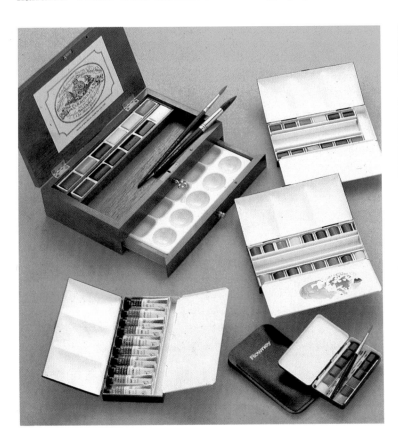

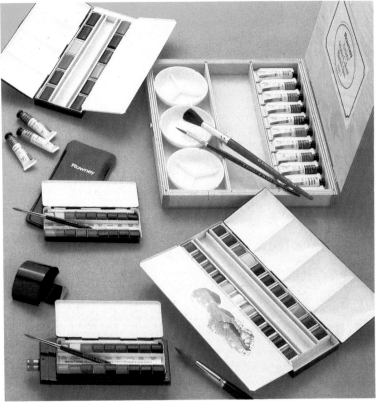

An example of a fine pen
drawing that could be
executed only on fine, smooth
paper.

Paper Watercolour paper comes in different weights and textures, so you have a good range from which to choose. A good medium paper is 60-pounds; at 200-pounds it approximates to cardboard. The surfaces of paper are known as 'hot-pressed', which is very smooth, 'not' (not hot-pressed), which is medium, and 'rough', which has a very marked tooth. Unless the paper is thick (above say 72-pounds) sketching blocks are not altogether suitable as the paper is apt to bubble up. Watercolour board, which sometimes goes under the name of fashion board, is usually smooth, and of excellent quality, suitable for all finishes. Cartridge paper is much cheaper than watercolour paper, but unless of good quality is inclined to let the user down, as it puckers up if there is too much water. You can use watercolour paper as it is, pinned to a drawing board, but the best method, though it may take a little extra time, is to 'stretch' it, not nearly so formidable as it sounds. Purists make use of a stretching frame, but far simpler is the method where you wet the paper, lay it on the drawing board face up, and tape it down with masking tape or brown adhesive tape (Scotch tape is all right but sometimes tears the paper immediately beneath it). When dry the paper will be drum-tight, a perfect working surface, and if need be the paper can be dampened slightly again before painting. Stretching is more necessary when the paper is light. A further short cut is to dampen the paper and fix it to the drawing board with spring clips (sold by art shops). For outdoor work where you may not need paper drawing-board size, a smaller panel of wood can suffice, and where you intend making several pictures you can put down several sheets of paper, wetting the top one in turn, painting on it, and then taking if off, leaving the others in the clip for further work.

When the picture is completed it is better to cut it out from the tape which is holding it to the drawing board. If the tape is pulled there is always the danger of tearing the paper and ruining the work. Of course, the adhesive or masking tape can be left on if the artist intends to frame the picture. If a mount is being used (as it really must be for a watercolour) the tape-covered edges of the picture will be hidden under the mount and provide more of an overlap for the part of the picture that is actually showing.

Drawing Board There is no substitute for a drawing board when painting in watercolours. If you wish to have a more resilient surface, you can place a pad of newspaper between the paper and the board. A *T-square* is an accessory to a drawing board that saves measuring up

when you are drawing horizons, and a *set-square* used in co-ordination with a T-square enables you to get verticals absolutely upright.

You will add other ingredients to your basic kit as you find them necessary, some of them obvious such as *pencils* (a variety from hard to soft), *pastels* (which mix if water-based), *dividers* and a pair of *compasses* (an intended circle which is not quite right sticks out like a sore thumb). Dividers are used to compare distances and are useful if the watercolour is to be meticulously accurate. *Blotting paper* can be very handy for soaking up a watercolour wash which has got out of hand, to take out areas (creating clouds in sky and waves in water) and to tone down colours. *Sponge* is also a help in evolving textures, taking out surplus water, and applying paint where the use of a brush is not suitable (where you want a mottled finish). A sponge can also be used instead of a large brush when applying water to the watercolour paper when it is being stretched prior to being worked on. For fine work, *cotton buds* are excellent for taking off surplus moisture in a very small area. Although there is not much mess associated with watercolours, household tissues and rags are useful.

You can use coloured inks in association with watercolour, therefore *pens* with nibs of dif-

Stretching paper is essential for achieving a final flat surface for a watercolour. You can either sponge the paper wet or leave it to soak in a sink or bath. It is advisable to cut the gum strip into appropriate lengths before you begin the stretching.

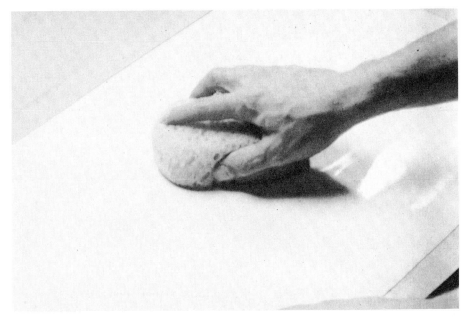

Soaking the paper.

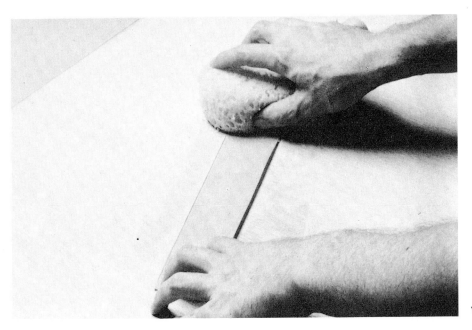

Wetting the pre-cut gum strip.

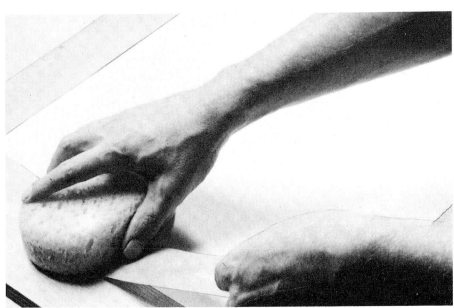

Applying the gum strip to the edge of the paper.

ferent sizes, *Indian* and *coloured inks* should all be kept in mind and within reach, as well as containers for water. Pens and nibs come in a very wide variety of shapes and sizes, ranging from mapping pens to lettering pens, the nibs of which often have reservoirs to hold the ink. Among the most useful are Rapidograph pens, which have a range of 'nibs' from 0.1 upwards. 0.1 is almost as fine as a spider's web. The great advantage of Rapidographs is the even line and the constant supply of ink provided by a cartridge, though those with a very fine point do have a tendency to clog after a while. Calligraphic fountain-pens with interchangeable units can be a great asset. Ordinary steel nibs, now mostly used in artwork and not for writing letters, have a limited life and if the points 'cross over' there is no point in trying to rescue them.

Erasers are a valuable accessory if they are not used too energetically, for damage may otherwise occur to the paper. Plastic erasers are the most versatile but, for charcoal, a putty rubber or a piece of bread is advisable. Erasers can not only be used to rub out intrusive pencil work but also to tone down the paint areas.

Applying a Wash The most important thing in watercolour painting is to know how to apply a wash. There is nothing easier. A wash is a smooth and even transparent tone of diluted colour. You need to have sufficient colour mixed, because you will rarely get the same tint again if you run out half-way. Use a large brush, fully loaded, and with the paper at modest slant (a book under the back of the drawing board is ample), carry the brushful of colour lightly across the top of the paper, left to right, or right to left, but keep the direction consistent. The wet colour will gently roll down like a wavelet, and when it gets to the bottom, or the place you want it to stop, mop off the surplus wash with a dry brush or blotting paper. If you want to graduate your colour, darker at the top, lighter at the bottom, you will add water to your brush after each line of wash so at the bottom you will be using almost pure water. This is excellent for skies. If you want washes darker at the bottom than the top, start with water and add the wash gradually or, alternatively, simply turn your paper upside-down. You can introduce washes of a different colour into a wash in progress, or even touches of pure colour from the tube or pan.

If you wish to apply a wash over a large area such as a sky it is advantageous to wet the paper beforehand with a sponge, waiting till it is just moist before applying the wash (you can hurry up the drying process by dabbing with a clean rag). Rough paper will take more water than smooth, and watercolour board least of all.

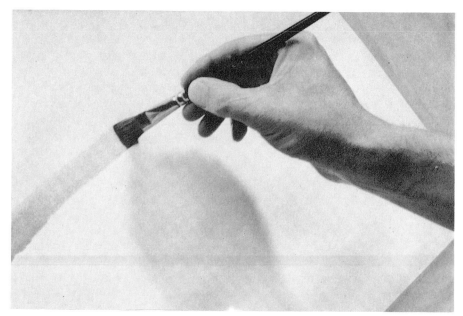

Applying paint with a fully loaded brush.

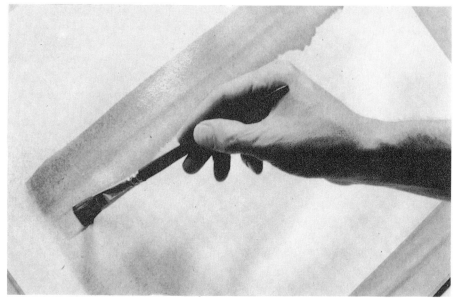

Applying the wash gradually.

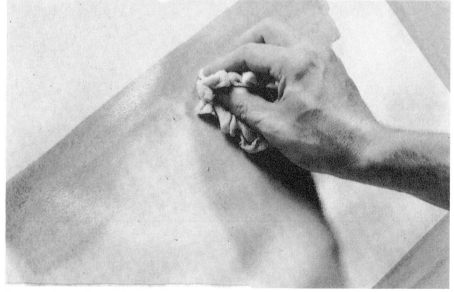

Dabbing with a soft rag or blotting paper.

A variety of different washes on a fairly coarse paper.

This interesting landscape (*below*) employs the techniques described in this part of the book.

Above: An Ancient Beech Tree,
by Paul Sandby, 1725–1809.

A full range of sable
watercolour brushes.

Far right: A selection of
watercolour papers:
1. RWS 90;
2. Green's Pasteless;
3. Whatman's Rough 200;
4. Fabriano NOT 90;
5. Whatman's HP 140;
6. Ingres;
7. Bockingford.

An example of what can be achieved by using Scotch tape. The artist has applied a piece of tape and then washed over it. The tape is then removed and placed in another position to repeat the process, thus producing this interesting tartan effect.

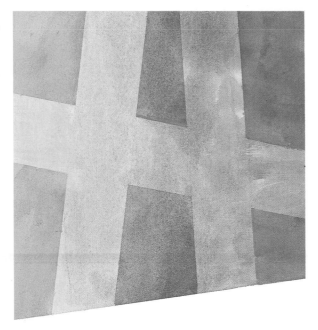

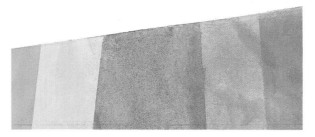

You can lay a wash over a small area, and the only thing to remember is to keep the direction of the brush strokes consistent, and never, for a wash, up and down, Once a wash has been applied, it is better to let it dry out thoroughly before doing anything else, and it is more effective to put strong washes over weak ones than the other way about. You can apply as many successive washes as you want, but after four or so there is a chance of them becoming lifeless as the watercolour paper begins to disappear. But of course it depends on what kind of picture you are painting. Many great artists have loaded wash upon wash. In art, nothing is firm and fixed, and if you do not want to do what someone says you should do, what does it matter? You are the person who is painting the picture.

Sometimes you may wish to lay an 'incomplete' wash, a wash where there are objects to be painted which are *lighter* than the wash. The beauty of the colour wash is that it is smooth. You do not want to go round the edges of anything. On the other hand, if this feature is to be lighter than the wash, there will be no way through the wash except by adding white to the mix and making it opaque. This is where masking fluid can be so invaluable. Masking fluid is a creamy sticky substance which, with a small soft brush, you paint on to the area you

do not wish to be covered by the wash. It rapidly becomes tacky, and then dry, and you can apply your wash over it. When the wash is dry, you peel off the masking fluid, either with the point of a knife or by rubbing it with the finger tips, whereupon it will come off like rubber solution. Beneath it the virgin paper will be ready to be painted on. Masking fluid is most suitable on smooth surfaces, as it is inclined to pick up fragments from rough or hairy paper. Do not rely too much on masking fluid. It is not a magic material.

When using watercolours it is always advisable to have at least three jars of water, one clean for light washes, one fairly clean, and a general purpose jar for washing out the brushes. If you are using a paint box with pans, there will always be certain pans with vestiges of other colours on them, as at some stage you will mix the colours on your brush rather than in a dish, especially if you are using the colours at full or moderate strength. It is a good idea to clean off the pan surfaces periodically, so that the colour is what it purports to be.

It is quite possible to paint a watercolour using washes only, and indeed many of the great watercolourists of the past have done just that, overlapping the washes to suggest shadow and distance and not needing anything stronger such as paint straight from the pan. Many of these early artists never used white as a colour, preferring to let the white of the paper show through for their highlights. This was known as 'the English style'. 'The French style', somewhat frowned upon, incorporated white paint – though it might be mentioned that the Chinese white found in most paint boxes is not a very powerful covering agent; process white or designers' white gouache is much more effective.

Most teach-yourself-painting books advise using watercolours light to dark, as opposed to oils where dark to light is reckoned the better. Of course you cannot make much of an impact with light washes over dark washes, even if they can be seen; but, despite all this, when using watercolours you can put the darks in first if the very dark colours are not used thickly. A wash of brown or diluted black can easily be modified when need be, though it may be necessary to dispel another taboo – that freshness is all in watercolours, and that the spontaneous touch is a must. This is not so. You can use the technique you want, and you can even modify the 'flat brush' technique of oil painting by rubbing the moist watercolour surface horizontally with the flat sable or nylon brush to get the same kind of texture you can achieve with oils. When you do this, naturally you will not be able to use the white of the paper; so you will use white gouache for your highlights.

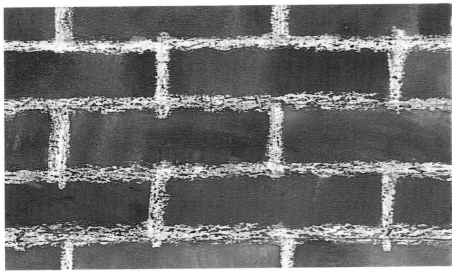

In this group, use of the wax-resist method is illustrated. A candle has been used to draw in portions of the pictures prior to actual painting.

Here the artist has chosen a picture postcard as his subject matter.

First of all, he has decided in his own mind what to put in and what to eliminate. Then he has drawn in the different areas in simple outline.

With the application of simple flat washes a feeling of distance is starting to emerge.

Some artists doing outdoor work prepare their paper beforehand with a colour wash – blue for sky, some dark colour for the ground – and no doubt it suits them. But it means that their imagination is restricted by what they have already down before them. They are being programmed to do a certain kind of picture. It is supposed to save drying time, as if five minutes or so makes any difference when sketching outdoors. A way to help watercolours dry more quickly is to add a little methylated spirit to the water. Or, if indoors, place the watercolour in front of a fire, preferably when the watercolour painting is on the drawing board as otherwise it might curl.

Watercolour straight from the pan or tube, with just enough water to make the paint flow easily, provides a satisfying counterpoint to washes already laid down. Watercolour paintings do not have to be loose and dreamy; they can be as tight and highly coloured as you like, and the textures can be worked up as diversely as in an oil painting, a prospect that would have horrified the 18th-century masters of the medium, especially those who worked to a formula and whose pictures now fetch big

money simply because of the art market. One of these archaic formulas was to tint the paper according to the mood of the picture – nearly always a landscape. A wash of Naples yellow or yellow ochre was applied for a sunny lyrical scene, and a wash of grey or natural tint gave the right sense of foreboding for an overcast scene. There is nothing against this dodge – in fact it can make sense today – but it should not become a habit.

Watercolour paint can be applied in any consistency you wish. There is no need to use washes at all, as you can build up the picture with colour directly from the pan. This can be applied in a number of ways; in little dots with the point of the brush – you do not have to use the same colour; in small diagonal strokes, known as hatching; in small diagonal strokes going first one way and then the other, building up a tiny mesh (cross-hatching); in little moist blobs so that the colours melt into those next to them. It is sometimes recommended that newcomers to watercolour painting should use only medium or large brushes, but this can take a lot of the fun out of experimentation and it may also not be the artist's kind of thing at all. Some

25

26

Far left: Shady Quiet, by Samuel Palmer.

Far left below: A Country Lane, by Thomas Gainsborough, 1727–1788.

Top left: Bridlington Harbour, by A. V. Copley Fielding, 1787–1855.

Bottom left: Norham Castle, Northumberland, by J. M. W. Turner.

people are born miniaturists who prefer to work on the smallest of scales, and if they are instructed to use large brushes and paint in a bold forthright manner they may never even find out where their talents lie. So if you wish to work in an area an inch square, go to it, and use a magnifying glass if it seems a good idea. Miniature sparkling pictures are just as 'good' (whatever that may mean) as big broad sketches.

Textures add interest to the picture surface, and there are many ways to achieve this. An interesting method is spattering the wash (still moist or dry) by loading a bristle brush with paint and running the fingers quickly through the bristles. You can put dots of colour by using a loaded decorator's brush and dabbing the tips of the bristles on to the surface. You can create the impression of foliage by dabbing at a green area with a sponge, blotting paper or tissues. A feathery texture can be achieved by holding a large brush, with not much paint on, close to the end of the bristles, and flicking the paper. The character of watercolour can be changed completely by being covered with blotting paper while still wet, and an even more drastic way is to immerse the watercolour in a bowl of water, swirl the paper slightly, take out, and treat with blotting paper. A watercolour which seems to be getting dull can be transformed by the use of pen-and-ink, pastel,

coloured pencils, and gouache. Gouache and true watercolour do not need to exist in self-contained compartments, but can be blended perfectly well on the same sheet of paper.

In laying a sequence of orthodox washes it *is* advisable to let each wash dry out in turn; however, remarkable effects can be obtained by painting wet-on-wet, guiding the changing colours with blotting paper. Paint straight from the pan can be put down moist, and then a loaded brush of water placed gently on top. Once again as you watch to see how chance is operating you have blotting paper or a tissue at the ready to control it. There is no way to predict how one colour will 'bleed' into another, but manipulating the transition takes away the element of chance.

There are so many ways of experimenting with watercolour that you will find your own method, and if you think you have discovered a winner go ahead with it despite failures, changing your brushes, changing the colours you are using, or turning to a different kind of paper. It is a far cry from the overlapping washes of the old masters, but they too were not averse to experiment, without having the variety of brushes, colours and papers that we have today.

All the methods described have been different ways of applying ordinary watercolour paint to the surface of the paper, but any

Right: A progression of illustrations in which masking fluid has been used. *Top:* Trees have been painted with masking fluid. *Middle:* A background wash has been applied. *Bottom:* Masking fluid has been removed and final details have been added.

Far right: Examples of different methods of applying watercolours.

Left: This interesting watercolour has been produced using the wax-resist method.

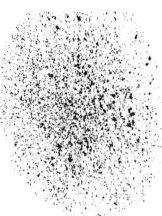

Flicking paint brush.

Dabbing with decorator's brush.

Dabbing over wash with tissue.

Dabbing dry wash with sponge.

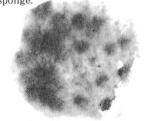

Dabbing wet wash with sponge.

outside medium, such as water-based pastels (or coloured pencils), is compatible with watercolour. By using the incompatibility of oil and water we can get amazing results. Mention has already been made of the techniques of using oil pastels in combination with watercolour, and this can be extended to using candle grease. If you stroke a candle across paper you will lay down a film, and when this is painted with watercolour the paint will slip off it or it will lie on top, unable to penetrate to the paper. Candle grease will not take the top off a wash, and further washes when applied will in all probability flow off it or settle uneasily on top, depending on how much candle grease you have put on. A further variation is pitting the layer of candle grease, either with a sharp object or by rubbing it with sandpaper. Where the paper is exposed the watercolour will take. Use the candle method with discretion; you are not making a candle-grease pie.

IS THE WATERCOLOUR WASH THE VERY FIRST STEP TO A PAINTING?

It can be – if for example you are going to have a large expanse of sky – but not necessarily. You may wish to outline your design on the white paper, and then put in the first wash. At the other extreme, you may not want to put in *any* design, not even rough pencil marks, to show what is going where.

If you want to do a watercolour painting which is virtually a tinted drawing you put all your detail in, either with a sharp pencil or pen and ink, remembering that if you want additional effect and the ink to 'bleed' into the watercolour you must use a non-waterproof ink.

A simple exercise which will give you a chance to try out a simple wash is a sea scheme

An effective painting has been achieved by using the simplest of washes.

with a ship. Draw a horizontal line about two-thirds of the way down the paper, used upright or lengthwise. Apply your wash of diluted blue (ultramarine or Prussian blue), darker at the top, and stop it at the horizon, using blotting paper or tissue. If it overlaps slightly it does not matter as your sea will be darker than your sky. Mix a sea-colour wash, using what seem to be appropriate colours; blue and green are the obvious ones, but add other colours, such as a brown and, for extra drama, a touch of black. Lay down your wash from the horizontal line, letting the water go to the bottom of the paper and there mopping up the surplus. At any stage during this wash you can add further colours.

If you wish to have clouds, prod at the blue wash while still moist with a pad of cotton wool. If you wish to have waves on the water, use the edge of a piece of blotting paper, picking out wave shapes, but not excessively, indicating rather than describing. You can mix a darker wash, perhaps brown with a touch of blue, and put in land on the horizon, adding variety by giving light and shade with a small piece of blotting paper or a cotton bud. If you want a darker piece of land use paint straight from the pan. Unless the land is going to be elaborate you can place this in without preliminary drawing, though the boat will probably have to be drawn in (or traced in). It is easier to have the boat on the horizon, straddling the horizon, or not far below it, because if it is near the bottom of the paper you will be looking down on it, and the boat shape will not be so evident to a viewer. If you are tracing a boat on to the paper bear its logical position in mind. If the sky is fairly light you will find that birds in white will not show up very clearly, though they will on a green/blue sea. You can pick the bird shapes out (a flat V) with blotting paper, adding a touch of black at the front end to indicate the head and beak. Or you can put the sea-birds in with opaque white paint, such as process white. It must be emphasized that the Chinese white found in paint boxes is *not* a very solid covering pigment.

A second simple picture can be made by using hills, a middle distance of trees and a pond in the foreground. As before, you put the horizon in, and you can then put in the whole of the sky, even over the part where the hills will come (the hill colour will go over the sky colour). For relatively simple shapes, you may not need to pencil in the outlines, or you may prefer to put them in using some kind of neutral tint and a pointed brush. The darkest area of the picture will be the line of trees between hills and pond, and you can experiment with reflections, adding tiny dots of pure colour to suggest people. Remember that reflections are always absolutely vertical. For the hill part, you can apply further washes to suggest where the light is falling, or you can take out some of the first wash with blotting paper. You can also use blotting paper to take out clouds (and reflections of clouds). In the line of trees, try not to make them too green, adding brown or red to cool the colour down.

If you wish to try your hand at more detailed work, put in grasses and reeds in the immediate foreground, suggesting that this is the limit of the pond, and you can use fairly strong colour for such features. When you have got the basic picture down, and are reasonably happy with it, do not be afraid to experiment. If you do not quite know *what* to put in, look through some illustrations; there will certainly be something suitable, and if you do not feel sufficiently confident to put in a detailed object try a blocked-in silhouette, remarkably effective against a background. From the start cultivate a spirit of adventure.

Below: This charming scene has been created by first painting in the background hills, middle distance trees and foreground pond. *Right:* Try practising details that can be used in the foreground as shown here.

Right and below: A gradual build up of washes (notice that areas of paper have been left open) for sky and clouds, finished with small applications of thicker white paint.

Far right, top: Here, the cloud formations are painted with thicker white paint on an overall blue wash.

Far right, bottom: A light wash, with subtle washes of darker colour for clouds, creates a dramatic, but not overworked, sunset effect. Notice how the 'edges' of the clouds are highlighted with yellow. It is important to remember that clouds are not flat; they have a form and will therefore react to light.

A simple seascape, using washes and flecks of white paint.

Manganese Blue

Sap Green

Cobalt Green

Vandyke Brown

Raw Sienna

Manganese Blue/Vandyke Brown

Sap Green/Cobalt Green

Vandyke Brown/Sap Green

A dramatic moorland landscape.

34

Plenty of colour and washes have been used to produce a slightly abstract landscape.

DRAWING AND PERSPECTIVE

The amount of preliminary drawing that goes into a watercolour depends on the artist. There may be a few scribbles indicating the approximate placing of the design, perhaps a few horizontal or vertical strokes, or the drawing may be realistic and exact and if necessary stand up by itself without any colouring. If you wish to do this kind of work, and nothing is more satisfactory than seeing a black-and-white picture gradually take on colour, you will need to know something about drawing techniques. These are not difficult, and the basic thing to remember is to draw what is there and not what you think is there. That is, if you want to produce a realistic drawing. You are not obliged to. You can put in an outline and colour what is inside it, as children do. An outline does not exist in nature; it is a convention which people who are drawing are obliged to use because they are interpreting a three-dimensional subject in two dimensions. What is an outline? It is a dividing line between areas which are light and areas which are darker.

In drawing all we have is outline and tone. Success is not dependent on manual dexterity – you are not playing the piano. It depends on looking and assessing, seeing how some shapes relate to other shapes and how light and dark they are with regard to each other. The shapes can be simple, looked at once, and put down with reasonable accuracy. It can be a barn in a field, or an apple on a tablecloth. Sometimes shapes can be complex, such as a face, but no matter what it is no shape is too difficult to depict on paper.

We do not have to know how the barn was built. All we see is a rectangle with a sloping angular shape on top (the roof). Depending on our viewpoint we may see part of the side of the barn, and the shadows will depend on where the sun is. The rectangle may be broken up by inner rectangles and squares – windows and doors – but although we know that they are these shapes they may not appear so. If the front of the barn is in part shadow, a window may show as merely a small horizontal splash of light where the sun picks out the window sill, leaving the rest in darkness. Or the window may appear as a small shapeless blob, where light is reflected from the glass. A door, which we know is a rectangle and which a child or primitive artist would put in as a rectangle, may be recognized by a dark shadow at the top, where the upper part of the door, slightly inset, is shadowed by the brickwork above.

Once it is appreciated that the outline is only a means to an end and that the effect of solidity

is more important than a line surrounding a white shape then a barrier is crossed. The effect of solidity is achieved by placing an object in space. It cannot be real space because paper is by definition flat, so we use the device known as perspective. There is nothing complicated about perspective. It is there about us all the time. You only have to lift your eyes from this page and look around you. Perhaps the television is in the corner, and the top of it will almost certainly be below eye-level. You will see that the top does not appear to be a perfect rectangle (even if it actually is), and that the two sides appear to move in towards each other. If the television set was 200 metres long the two sides would most probably appear to meet, though we know full well that they do not.

If you look along a straight road in the direction of the horizon the road appears to narrow; a person walking down this road seems to get smaller, losing height at the same rate as the road narrows. If there are telegraph poles alongside it they will appear to shrink, and if you draw an imaginary line connecting the bases of the poles and another connecting the tops of the poles you will find that these meet on the horizon. The only time to see a true horizon is at sea, where the sky meets the water, for a horizon has nothing to do with the skyline. If you were in the Alps the skyline would be way above you. The horizon would be

Right: This diagram explains perspective visually. The road seems to disappear into infinity. The figures, houses and telegraph poles recede to the points of convergence, the vanishing point.

An example of
perspective drawing. Note that
where the lines converge is the
vanishing point.

behind the mountains, at eye-level. For that is
where the horizon is, at eye-level.

Objects above or partly above the eye-level
appear to go down towards the horizon and
those below appear to go up. If you look at the
roof of a house from any position except
straight on you will see it meekly obeying the
laws of perspective, and if you draw another
imaginary line it will lead to the horizon at what
is known as its vanishing point. If there is more
than one roof, and each is pointing in a
different direction, as in a higgledy-piggledy
village, you will see that every roof leads to the
horizon, but each roof has its own vanishing
point. There is only one horizon in a scene, but
any number of vanishing points.

Right: Lonely Dell, Wharfedale
by J. M. W. Turner. An
example of a watercolour
where the correct use of
perspective plays an
important part.

Cayne Waterfall, North Wales.
A brilliant almost effortless
portrayal of cascading water
by Thomas Girtin.

Above: Castle Point, York, by John Warwick Smith, 1749–1831. Never so strong as those of Towne, Smith's watercolours nevertheless received lavish praise in his day.

Left: Killarney and Lake, by William Pars, 1742–1782.

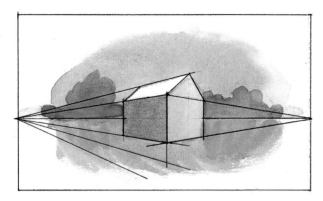

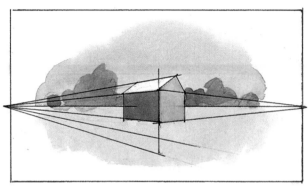

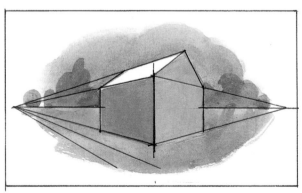

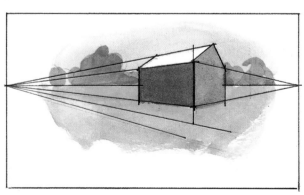

Without perspective a drawing or a painting will be flat, and by using perspective you obtain solidity and recession. Objects 'out there' will be laid out in their own kind of space. The horizon can be as high or as low in a drawing as you wish – it can even be off the top of the paper, but objects still recede towards it. Sometimes perspective can be tampered with to get dramatic effects (Salvador Dali was a master at this) and the experts at perspective are not artists but architects. Their perspective has to be right, whereas if an artist's perspective *looks* right that is all that matters. Playing with perspective can be fun and if you use two perspectives in the same picture it can be startling.

Although the ancient Romans knew about perspective, and used it in their murals, the secret seems to have been lost (or just ignored) and when it was rediscovered (or reissued) a few hundred years ago many artists painted pictures just to display their cleverness. And sometimes cleverness is needed, for all things, including human figures, have to obey the rules. If a person extends a clenched fist towards you it will appear enormous, sometimes larger than the rest of the person. And even objects which we do not associate with having solidity, such as clouds, have to follow the rules. That is why some clouds in pictures appear flat and un-interesting; they are merely put on as blotches with maybe a bit of shading beneath them. Of course you do not have to measure everything up; the main thing is to get the effect of perspective, not whether the interpretation is 100 per cent accurate. No one is going to award you a prize for being exceptionally good at perspective drawing; perspective is something to use, to manipulate.

Every law, of course, is made to be broken. And so we come to accidental vanishing points. Surfaces which are tilted sometimes converge on vanishing points which lie below or above the eye-level. If you hold a sheet of card at a slant you will see that its vanishing point alters as you move the card around. A good example is seen in a road going uphill, when the sides will appear to converge at a point above the horizon, or below the horizon if the road goes downhill.

You can gauge sizes by how objects appear in perspective. An object twice as far away from the viewer as another identical object appears to be half as tall; if it is three times as far away it seems one-third as tall; four times as far away a quarter as tall, and so on, and so on. This can be quite useful when putting in items to illustrate the scale of something.

Aerial perspective has nothing to do with what it might seem – perspective from above. It

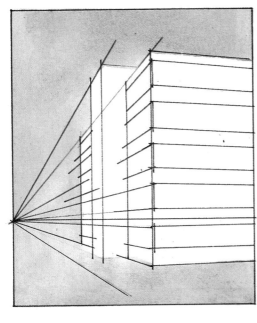

Some examples of a few of the
many problems which can
arise in perspective drawing.

is about atmosphere. Dust and moisture are inclined to obscure the more distant objects, and the further away something is the less distinct and the lighter in tone it will appear. This is of more interest to watercolour painters than those who are making a drawing. The effect of distance can be reproduced in a drawing by very light or broken and dotted lines; in a watercolour by the use of bluish tints. This was used as a formula by 18th- and 19th-century watercolourists whether or not the distance appeared blue.

It is all very well reading about perspective, but does it work for you? It is a good idea to go out and look at a few buildings and begin sketching them. How do you start? The first thing to do is to put in your horizon. If you are not quite certain where this is, extend your fist with the thumb uppermost until it is on the level of your eye. You can then put in pre-liminary lines, casually, setting the scene, put in lightly, and then build up on these until you find a place on the paper which you think will be a good starting point. It may be the angle of a wall, it may be a doorway, it may be where the walls reach the roof, and once you have established one or two set points you can begin building up the drawing, altering the preliminary lines as you go along. There is no need to rub them out; just go over the top of them with a more determined and blacker line.

There is no necessity to complete the drawing if you do not wish to; concentrate on the parts that interest you, and if for example you find the windows and window surrounds particularly fascinating do these and forget the rest of the building or leave it incomplete. You may care to put in the individual bricks or stones, but there will probably be more of them than you think and a suggestion of brickwork is sufficient.

Landscape and Townscape

Landscape and townscape are the most popular forms of art, and in any exhibition of amateur work landscapes will outnumber everything else many times to one, with maybe flower paintings coming second.

There are several reasons for this popularity. Landscapes are there, and do not need to be arranged. You can pick your vantage point, and select only what you want to put in. There may be elements in the landscape which you may feel are too technically demanding; there may be a country scene with an old farm cart, and the open wheels may present a problem. You can ignore such objects either by omitting them from the view or looking elsewhere. Always draw or paint something which is of interest to you, and if landscapes bore you there are plenty of other subjects.

A further point about landscapes is that they are motionless, and you can spend as much or as little time on them as you wish. Naturally there are changes of light, and the shadows will alter, but at a fairly slow rate. Unless you are a very slow worker you are not likely to be caught on the hop by changing shadows, though weather changes are a different matter and what could be a charming scene with sharp lighting effects which pick out the detail can turn into a dull monotonous view with nothing much happening at all.

It is never fruitful to do anything just for practice. Some experts advise a newcomer to watercolour to make a series of small squares of different colour washes just to see what they look like and to get to know the contents of the paintboxes. It is difficult to imagine anything more tedious. The owner of the paintbox knows what the colours are; they are sometimes marked if there is any doubt. And it is much more interesting to see the colours in action. Sometimes there will be miscalculations, but what does that matter?

You may not be willing to hand out your early try-out efforts for others to see, but always keep your work even if it does not come up to expectations, for at some later stage you may fancy reworking it, using it as a base for a fictitious picture. And if you are making drawings with a view to turning them into watercolours, bear in mind that a relatively tame scene can be transformed with colour. Make written comments on the drawing about the colours you see if you do not have your paintbox with you, and as you do this you will find that you are analysing the scene afresh, looking at it in a new way. Maybe there is a yellow cornfield and you may think that the hedges which border it could be 'brought out' by making the colour and tones extra strong.

Far left: The buildings appear to recede into the distance because stronger colour has been used in the foreground.

Far left, below: An example of aerial perspective.

The same scene painted four times, using different colours to indicate changes of mood and season.

When choosing a landscape you should first decide what the main theme of the picture will be. The paintings on these two pages show (*far left*) where the foreground and, in the other, where the distance predominates.

43

Far left above: Lincoln by Peter de Wint. Using only two brushes, both large, one pointed, the other stubby, de Wint was able to achieve either a finesse of detail or a sweeping bold wash.

Far left below: Greta Bridge, (1805), by J. S. Cotman.

Left: Wood Scene (1810) by John Crome

46

Top left: Having decided upon his subject, the artist has carefully worked out his composition and has decided to place a large tree in the foreground to give depth to his painting.

Bottom left: The painting springs to life as simple areas of colour blocked in with flat washes are applied. It is at this stage that the tonal quality of the finished picture will become apparent.

Below: The painting has now reached an exciting stage. With accurate drawing and carefully thought out perspective, the artist can now confidently work into his picture in the knowledge that his problems have been solved in the first two stages.

Left: Detail.

Overleaf: At this advanced stage the artist is concerned solely with detail. Note carefully how he has used various techniques and effects, such as stippling, to create the shapes of the trees and how convincing the wooden cladding of the barn appears.

47

The finished painting.

Figure and Pool
by John Singer Sargent, 1856–1925.

A watercolour and pencil sketch of clouds by John Constable. The sky is the keynote, the standard of scale, and the chief organ of sentiment.

*Summer Day, New
England* by Maurice
Prendergast, 1859–1924.

Woman Sewing by
Winslow Homer, 1836–1910.

Painting a townscape highlights all the problems of perspective in the drawing of buildings, cars and people.

When you are looking at a landscape it may be a problem deciding where the 'edges' come, where the picture should begin and end. An easy solution to this can be a homemade viewfinder which is nothing more than a piece of card with a rectangular hole cut in the middle. Alternatively the viewfinder of a camera can be used. And it is always worthwhile to bear in mind that pictures can be vertical (known as 'portrait' shape) instead of horizontal ('landscape' shape).

This will help not only in composition but also in relating the elements to each other, helping you to see in tones rather than shapes. Sometimes tones seem to be much of a muchness, and it is advantageous to half-close the eyes, so that although the detail is lost the broad masses are more easily differentiated.

When drawing landscape, and indeed anything else, put down what you can see and not what you know is there. If there is detail it should be in the foreground. Trees are most likely to be a stumbling block to the newcomer to landscape drawing and painting, and it is very easy to make them symmetrical, with the boughs and branches distributed in an even pattern. Mostly they are not. All artists have different ways of doing trees, and some of them try to put on every leaf, which can be a long laborious job. A suggestion of leafiness is better, with the awareness that leaves occur in clusters and masses. What might at first appear to be changes of colour are in fact changes of tone, due to the fact that some leaves are in the light and some in the dark, and some are in the

shadow of other leaves. In drawing this can be expressed in shading and in watercolour painting by adding a 'shadow colour' to the basic 'local' colour. So if you are using a medium green for leafage you would add a darker colour to the mix (it is immaterial what it is as it depends on what general colour scheme you are using); you would not use a different kind of green for the darker parts. The trunks of trees are much easier to do than leafage, and it is important to make them seem solid by using shading. And often trunks are leaning slightly to one side, especially if they are single trees in an exposed place. Study how other painters do their trees; you will find incredible variety. A short cut to putting in leaves is to use a sponge doused in colour, not too wet, so that by applying the sponge lightly you can lay down an arrangement of little flecks. You can add shadow colours while the paint on the paper is still damp.

If you intend to use trees and tree parts in the foreground of the drawing or painting take some typical branches home and draw them there. You can then arrange where the light falls rather than by leaving it to nature.

Grass may present a slight problem. Except in the immediate foreground the blades of grass cannot be picked out individually and grass is best expressed by shading or in painting by using a 'shadow colour' in the mix. Tufts have a shaded side and cast shadows onto the ground. In the middle distance grass is best represented by graduating the tone as the ground rises and falls.

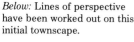

Below: Lines of perspective have been worked out on this initial townscape.

Much that applies to landscape applies to townscape too; never imagine details which you cannot see; observe and do not assume; always put your horizon in at an early stage; and do not necessarily count all the bricks. Townscape is unquestionably easier than landscape, though there are one or two extra things to remember such as always keeping your verticals absolutely upright. A building which is even slightly askew will look silly. If you have difficulty in drawing verticals use a setsquare, with the bottom of the paper as your horizontal.

In these days some people will think twice about venturing into a city armed with a sketchpad. So go in your car, and do your sketching from there, with the windows closed and the doors locked if necessary, preferably on a Sunday when you can park easily by the side of the road. If you feel like venturing out on foot the choice is yours.

Below: The painting begins to come alive with the use of some simple washes.

Bottom: The second stage before detail is added.

53

The finished painting. Note how each area has been simply blocked in with only the minimum of detail yet the overall impression is of precision and accuracy.

Townscapes can look unnatural without people, and often a few briefly sketched-in figures can bring life to city streets. They can also give scale to the buildings. If you want to put in a fairly large number of people, either singly or in groups, draw in 'perspective lines' so that the people will fit in, not too small, not too large. If there are no people in the sketch at all, take an object in the foreground of known size, perhaps a doorway, or maybe a parked car. Place a figure there and see if it looks right. Then take a rule, place the edge at the top of the head of the inserted figure and draw a line to a vanishing point, perhaps the one you have used for the principal buildings. Then do the same with the feet, so you have two converging

lines to the horizon. At any point along this route you can place a person of the appropriate size relative to the rest of the picture. Naturally you do not want the people in the same line as if they were standing in a queue; so you fit in people across the paper, making certain that they are in scale, which is easily done by looking directly across at the distance between the upper converging line and the lower and seeing that the people fit between them. The figures need not be specific; they can be suggested with a well-placed slash of paint, lightening the top to suggest a face (faces do not have to be put in in pink, as novices often do).

When putting optional extras in, such as a

Similar and even greater
problems of perspective,
inherent in the townscape of
the previous pages, are
experienced here.

few extra people, remember that they too have shadows which must run the same way as the shadows of the other objects. Groups of people can often be represented by a rough rectangle with blobs (the heads) on. Legs are often not seen when there are strong shadows. Townscapes can also be made realistic by including cars and other vehicles, parked and moving; and when using watercolour they can be used as accents of pure colour (just as artists of yesteryear used post boxes). If you draw a car from memory you may find it an odd experience. You will perhaps overemphasize the upper part of the car, and will almost certainly overestimate its height. In a street scene with pedestrians and traffic, heads will always be well above the roofs of cars. When next out, take a look at the windows of cars. Are they opaque? Can you see

through them? These factors depend on what lighting there is and from what direction it comes. The same applies to other solid scenefillers – the bus and the coach. If the wheels of cars and other vehicles seem to present a problem remember that a good part of them is in deep shadow and a suggestion of 'wheeliness' is often all that is necessary. If you cannot draw any kind of curvature try using the side of a coin; the aim is to indicate the presence of a wheel, not to draw up a set of blueprints for a motor manufacturer.

Of course both landscapes and townscapes can be tackled directly, using the point of the brush as a drawing instrument to lay in the basic design. But without some kind of framework, even just a squiggle or two in pencil, the straight-in approach using brush and paint can

A complete contrast to
the city scene of the
previous pages; only a
minimal amount of detail has
been employed in this
landscape.

Far left, middle and bottom:
A continuous progression of
tonal washes will bring the
picture to its finished state.

be hazardous without experience and the result can be a mess, with splodges of colour merging into each other. When you are using watercolour directly, think before you apply the paint. Have some idea what you are going to put down.

Landscapes can be approached using pencil and paint together, building the picture up little by little. The watercolour can be applied in sectional washes, and the pencil work can be put in on top of this, with more watercolour used to finish it off. Pen and ink can also be used, with the ink blending in with the wash. If pencil is used it can be erased when all the watercolour has been applied, though the eraser may remove a little of the paint surface, usually without any detrimental effect. If you propose to carry out this method always use good quality watercolour paper; it is very easy to take the top off inferior paper.

Above: Final washes and a little more detail complete the picture.

The photograph *(top left)* was used as a reference for the above picture.

Basic shapes are sketched in lightly in pencil *(centre left)*.

The artist has used masking fluid to indicate the stonework detail *(bottom left)*. After the initial washes have been applied and have dried the masking fluid has been removed.

In the final stages *(above)* the white lines of the stonework have been lightly washed over to give a more realistic effect and the picture is now finished.

Working from a colour transparency. Notice how the artist has altered the 'wide angle' look of the original and made the perspective more realistic.

Far right: A chart of colours which have been used to make this interesting study.

Manganese Blue

Manganese Blue/Vandyke Brown

Vandyke Brown

Vandyke Brown/Purple Lake/Cadmium Red

Cadmium Red

Purple Lake

Sap Green/Cobalt Green

Raw Sienna/White

63

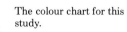
The colour chart for this study.

Manganese Blue

Windsor Blue

Olive Green

Gamboge Yellow

Hooker's Green

Permanent Mauve

Burnt Sienna

Neutral Tint

The wax-resist method was used on the tree trunks in this watercolour; it clearly helps to demonstrate the effect of strong sunlight in a tropical setting.

Figure Studies and Portraits

If you want to improve your drawing the classic way is to draw – and paint – the human figure. Most of the great artists of the past have done so, for the human figure is the most challenging of all subjects. No two people are the same; no two poses are the same. As, by and large, people are unwilling to take their clothes off to be drawn – and those who are willing probably cannot stay still – it will probably be necessary to enrol at an art school or join an art group (many art groups employ their own models). Fees are low, especially at evening classes run by the local community. The classes usually last two hours; much of the time is devoted to one or at the most two poses, but most teachers towards the end of the period go in for 'quickies'; five or ten minute poses in which there is just enough time to sketch in the basics.

Some people who have just started drawing and painting fight shy of going to life classes, feeling that they will be embarrassed, or, worse, make a fool of themselves by incompetence. There is no need to be diffident, of course, as nearly everyone feels nervous at first. Many people who go find that they can learn from fellow students as well as from the teachers. These teachers are tactful and helpful and the stuffy, autocratic art teacher, usually found not in art colleges but in second-rate schools is a comic figure from the past.

All styles and methods, all kinds of medium, straightforward and weird, are common at life classes. As an art student in the early 1950s the author was once asked in perfect seriousness if he was drawing the figure in 'the Egyptian style'. He was not, he was just experimenting with the new wonder of the age, coloured pencils in three million different shades. The emphasis of this book is on fun and pleasure, but please think seriously about life classes as they offer great opportunities of widening your artistic experience.

It is easiest to start off with drawing rather than painting. The drawings can be a base for watercolours when you get home, but until you get some experience in reproducing a person in two dimensions a pencil, pen, or length of charcoal are the best to begin with. You will be standing up to draw, so you will need a drawing-board (easels are usually supplied by the art college). It is a good idea to use a large sheet of paper, for you will find that if you are working on a small sheet legs and arms most probably will not fit in.

There are numerous ways of beginning a drawing of the nude, but it must always be remembered, as with landscape, that you are drawing what you see, not what you know is

This effective study has been painted directly from life with no preliminary work.

When drawing faces in watercolour it is always a good idea to practise the individual features first. Try to use form rather than lines to build up your shapes.

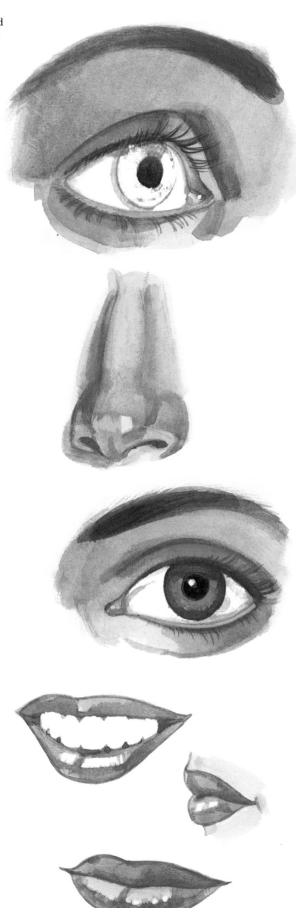

there. For example, anyone can draw a mouth freehand. But when actually looked at, a mouth may be seen as a shadow beneath the lower lip. Similarly with a nose. In certain light, a nose can only be detected by the shadow of it on the cheek. Old style books on drawing the nude spend half the time on anatomy, and why certain bones are there and why others are not. Muscles were regarded as important though they look no more interesting than elastic bands. You are not a surgeon about to cut somebody up. We are not about to draw skeletons so we can take it that they influence the shape and movements of the body. The proportions of the body are much more useful: a man is about eight heads tall, a woman six heads, a one-year-old child four heads; the halfway point down a man is the crutch. Fashion designers have their women eight-and-a-half heads tall, mainly to emphasize the legs, so physical facts can be manipulated if it suits the purpose. The shape of a man's torso is an equilateral (equal sided) triangle on one of the points.

An especially tricky point for newcomers is putting the head on the shoulders in a convincing manner. The neck does not sit on top of the shoulders, but is slightly below. A man's neck slopes slightly outwards (reading from the top), a woman's neck slopes slightly inwards. Hands and feet may present problems (even to important artists – look at Turner's figures and have a quiet chuckle). The hand is not all in one plane; the thumb lies below if the hand is held casually and not outstretched. In the foot, the ankle has to be exactly placed otherwise it looks like a frogman's flipper.

Where do you start? It is up to you. You can begin by putting in a rough outline, amending as you go along, putting in some guiding shadows; shadows are shapes which have no meaning and do not have to be interpreted. Some artists prefer to start by putting in the background shadows, 'bringing out' the figure against them. Or you can start with the head, working down from it; the eyes are a favourite place, as once in it is easy to begin sketching out the other features, and the eyes have the advantage of being set halfway down the head. Once the eyes are in, the ears can be put on. If the head is straight on without being bowed or tilted, the tops of the ears are on the same level as the eyes.

Build up with a mixture of line and tone, lightly pencilling in possible shapes and then going over them later when you are certain that they are reasonably accurate. Compare different shapes. Put out tentative scribbles where they may be. If there is a solid piece of torso such as the buttocks and thighs seen at an odd angle,

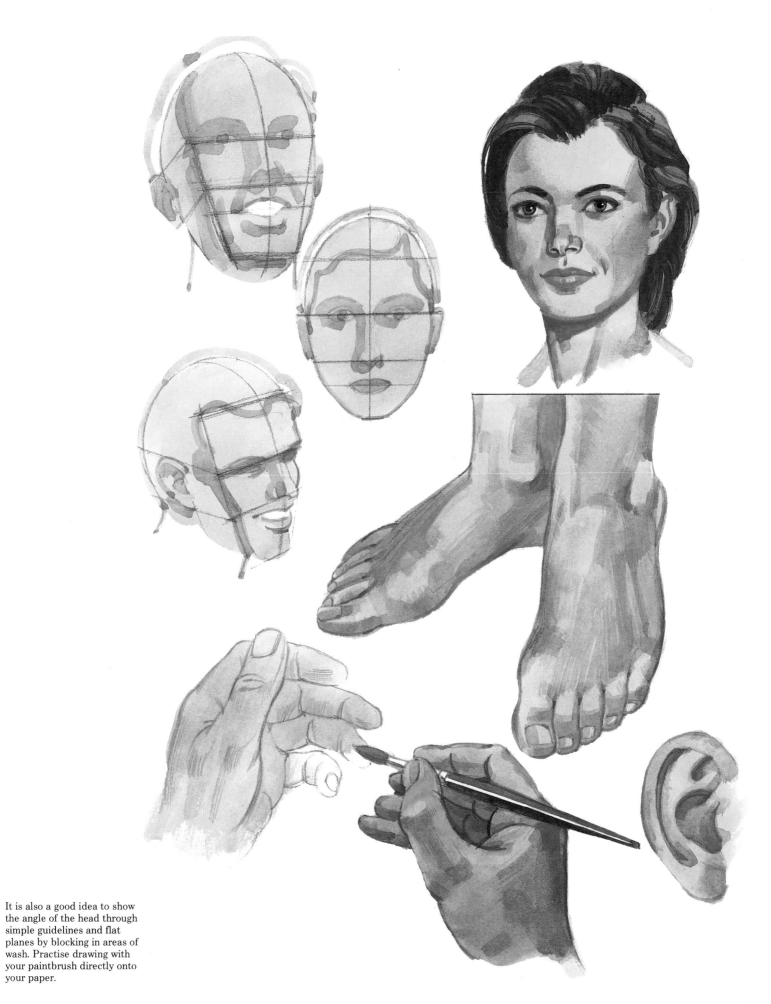

It is also a good idea to show the angle of the head through simple guidelines and flat planes by blocking in areas of wash. Practise drawing with your paintbrush directly onto your paper.

do that before tackling the subleties of the arms and legs. The only thing which is not advised is to start at the hands and feet and work inwards.

The effect of solidity is more important than physical accuracy. Do the legs look as though they are made of plywood? Look at the shadows. Look at the shadow below the knee and the slight protruberance of the knee bone. The ankle may only be indicated by the semi-circular shadow beneath it. And what is the drawing-pin in the middle of the stomach? Ah, the navel. It has been put in because the artist knows it is there, though all that can be seen of it is the merest shadow.

Once you have made progress with pencil or charcoal, bring in the paints. Watercolour is ideal for nudes, because the white paper coming through a pale orange or pale brown can evoke a marvellous skin colour. You can use the paint in washes over the pencil sketch; there is no need to stop the wash where the pencil line stops. You are not a child filling in a drawing in a colouring book. Outlines, as we have seen, are a convenience. Build up more washes if you wish, adding 'shadow colour' where necessary. Or you can use pencil and watercolour at the same time, a few suggestive lines here, a splash of paint there, a little grey to indicate back-ground shadow; there is no end to the possibilities. Or you can go straight in with colour, sketching the figure in outline in a very light colour, and amending it as you go along, building up flesh tints, adding shadows when appropriate, providing a background when you feel that you are on the right track (if you are wrong you can use a sponge and take the background out). Another way is to put the background in first, and then, using a brush loaded with water, 'fix in' the figure before beginning to apply colour. If the background colour is beginning to seep too much into the figure, take it out with a small piece of blotting paper, sponge, or a cotton bud. If the picture, although reasonably 'like', is turning out wishy-washy or faded, add more colour, or perhaps bring in coloured pencils, inks, or pastels.

There is no best 'one way' to draw the figure or paint it. There are dozens of approaches. It may need a good deal of concentration, but if you can apply a wash, if you can handle a pencil, if you can differentiate between high tones, low tones, and middle tones and can draw a distinction between what you see and what you think you see, there is nothing more satisfying. And if you can draw or paint a figure you can paint almost anything.

These delightful wash drawings owe their freshness and spontaneity to the fact that very little preparation has been made beforehand. Note that any guidelines can be erased once the watercolour has dried.

Experience in drawing the nude is a great help in drawing clothed figures. Folds in clothing fall into four categories – in hanging, pulled, heaped, and crushed materials. Folds are expressed by shading, but only put in those which are important. Clothing can be painted in one tone, and the shadows added afterwards in two tones, one for background shadows, one (stronger) for cast shadows. Pattern and texture should be put in discreetly as otherwise they will dominate the picture to the detriment of the figure.

The ability to draw and paint portraits is one of the most envied of talents. As with drawing the nude, it is important to observe and draw and paint what you see, not what you know is there. The outline of the face can be put in first, but it is more sensible to start with a fixed feature such as the eyes, or to put in the background shadows first. The great advantage of doing a portrait is that you have a model on the spot – yourself – and that you have an ace critic near at hand – your nearest and dearest. The eye is halfway down the head, for instance, and other useful dimensions are: the distance between the top of the forehead and the top of the nose is about the same as that between the top of the nose and the bottom of the nose. The distance between the top of the upper lip and the bottom of the chin is about the same as that between the top of the ear and the bottom of the ear. A good rendering of the eye is a key to a successful portrait; it is often forgotten that it is in three parts – the eye itself, the eyebrows, and the eyelids. When doing the eye, always put in a highlight, but make certain that it appears in the same place in both eyes.

The easiest pose is three-quarter, perhaps the most difficult is the profile. Up-tilted and down-tilted heads do not present problems if you remember about perspective and foreshortening. Even non-professional models can usually keep their heads still, but if you are doing a fully worked out portrait it is sometimes wise to take a Polaroid photograph to establish the pose if a coffee break is taken.

If you have become skilled in drawing and painting nudes and faces, you will have few problems with drawing animals, except that at any time an animal can suddenly move and will rarely go back to its original position. Many professional wildlife artists keep a collection of stuffed animals and birds. Quick sketches are often more satisfactory than fully worked out pictures, whether they are done in pencil, charcoal, pastel, or paints. Animals with the same all-over texture in their coats and fur are easier to do than those where there is a mix. Textures can be depicted in many ways: by using the point of the brush and making a

A selection of watercolour portraits. It is essential when painting portraits in watercolour to ensure that one does not muddy the colour but places washes that are not disturbed.

series of close dots; by hatching; by using a sponge; by using overlapping washes; and by representing hairs with lines drawn side by side with a thin nib. Changes of tone are more important than changes of colour. It is useful to remember that the torso and legs of many animals are contained in a perfect square.

The simplest kinds of creature to draw are those which can be taken in at a single glance, such as rodents, where the texture of the fur is consistent. Because of their bright colouring, birds are often the subject of watercolour artists, but it must be remembered that the feathers are in groups, each overlapping other feathers and throwing shadows, and the practice of adding single feathers with a short dab of the brush may not be convincing.

Still Life

The kind of painting which allows delicate gradations of tone is typified by the still life. This can be imaginary – it is no difficult matter to visualize bottles, jars, and the odd apple or lemon – or from life. Bottles are useful as they have highlights, which appear on the same side as the light source.

The simplest kind of still-life painting is carried out by covering the whole paper with a tint, then sketching objects in roughly with a pencil, charcoal, or the point of a brush. The paper will still be slightly moist, so do not worry if the outline design (if done with the brush) bleeds into the background. Then, using a medium wash for each object, making certain that the colours do not clash too much, fill in the objects, defining the bottle shapes, jars and fruit. This should not take long, and before the paint is too dry take out the highlights of the various items with a damp brush, again not worrying if the colour slops over. For darker objects, apply further washes, either of the same colour or some other, skirting round the highlights you have put in. If the paper is still moist, this helps merge the colours.

You now have four tones, including the highlights, and you provide a fifth, with shadow, which need not necessarily be black. Brown plus blue makes an excellent shadow mix. You can leave the outlines fairly loose if you wish, or you can tidy them up, either by applying further washes on the objects, applying a further wash on the background, using a small brush to run along the edge of the bottles, or you can tidy up by using a wet brush and taking off the wash where it has leaked over into an adjacent area. You can use white for the highlights rather than the white of the paper. This, of course, is the traditional light-to-dark method.

Rather than start off again, you can take off the paint with a wet sponge, or put the paper under a tap, so that you have the merest skeleton of your original watercolour painting. You can then go from dark-to-light, putting in your shadows first, your next darkest tints, and so on back to the background, putting in highlights with white paint last of all. If you are used to oil painting this method will come easily. For the whole of the painting you can make do with one brush, a medium about number three, pointed.

After inanimate objects, it is tempting to be more ambitious and try flowers. These are more difficult than bottles and jars, but you can bluff your way through by giving impressions of flowers rather than portraits, using dabs of muted colour on a slightly moist paper. If you are anxious to do justice to the flowers, look at them closely; what might at first glance appear

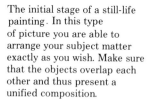

The initial stage of a still-life painting. In this type of picture you are able to arrange your subject matter exactly as you wish. Make sure that the objects overlap each other and thus present a unified composition.

The still-life arrangement
carefully sketched out.
In a watercolour it is most
important to leave all
highlights as blank paper. This
is particularly difficult in a still
life.

The finished painting.

Watercolour lends itself particularly to flower painting. Start by sketching in the basic composition.

Remembering to leave highlights, continue to lay your washes from light to dark. More precise detail can be added in the final stages to bring the picture to life.

to be a colour change may turn out on closer examination to be the shadow of one petal on another, so you do not modify the colour you are using, but add a slightly darker colour to the wash or try taking off part of the wash with a damp brush. It is sometimes worthwhile analysing certain flowers, seeing how a rose is in the form of a spiral, and how even a flower such as a pansy is not merely a symmetrical group of petals around a centre. The spontaneous approach really does pay off in flower pictures; if you do flower paintings too tightly you are in unwitting competition with the professional botanical artists, and you (and most professional painters) will soon realize your shortcomings. Roughing in flowers with a pencil can often be more of a hindrance than a help; you may well find yourself running out of space when you have miscalculated the distance between bloom A and bloom B, while if you are drawing with the point of a brush or just putting in blotches of likely colour you amend and adjust as you go along. You can let the flower colours run into each other, but it can be very tiresome if the greens infiltrate the rose pinks or snapdragon yellows.

In flower arrangements some of the leaves will be in deep shadow, and it is often a good idea to emphasize these shadowed leaves, even exaggerating them, so that the main flower colours stand out. The actual painting of a flower group can be carried out either light-to-dark or dark-to-light.

Flower paintings are a good introduction to indoor scenes. These do not have to have every item picked out as if for an auctioneer's catalogue, and you can keep some objects in mysterious shadow. It is an interesting process, working out how much you can suggest with a square of colour or a couple of verticals. For those who regard their paintings as a visual diary there is something uniquely satisfying in having a portrait of the interior of a well-loved room, and although interiors do pose a challenge it is one well worth taking up.

Many of the characteristics associated with interiors are shared by life paintings, in particular getting the perspective and the foreshortening right. It is vital to get the eye-level set in accurately, and as you will have objects which straddle the eye-level you will have parts of these objects appearing to go up and others down. The vanishing points of the boundary line between walls and ceiling should be worked out; they will rarely fall within the scope of the picture. The same goes for the division between walls and floors, You will probably not get floor area and ceiling area in together, but even so it is useful to know what their vanishing points are. Getting these right will establish the correct

dimensions of the room. There is no need to accentuate the wall/ceiling wall/floor dividing line heavily as a preliminary step. Roughly sketching it in is sufficient.

It is often more satisfactory to paint direct without pencil outlines, using the point of the brush to establish where things are and getting the tones in, leaving any detail to a later stage. It is easier if there is just one light source, either a window or a light. With a standard lamp or table lamp you can establish where you want your light source – in other words you can pose your interior to suit yourself.

As with still life and flower arrangements, one advantage of the interior is that it does not move around, and you can spend as much time on it as you like – unless you are using natural light from a window, which of course will mean that the shadows are constantly altering. In doing interiors, you can explore to the full the possibilities of direct painting, and as you become more adept you can create more difficult problems, for example using additional light sources or putting in a mirror.

If you are painting direct and are aiming for effect rather than an inventory, use a rough paper where detail is difficult to put down. With rough paper it is important to dampen it first, for otherwise you will find that the paint is adhering to only part of the surface. This creates a sparkling effect as there is a good deal of paper exposed, and if you want this by all means leave the paper dry.

If you go to an exhibition of amateur artists you will find very few interiors. They *are* more difficult than the ordinary open-air landscape, but they can be no less satisfying. You may find that you have a high ratio of failures in painting direct without pencil guide-lines. If you are in a sketching club and painting outdoors you may not want these failures exposed, while if you are painting interiors you can happily discard them (or wash them off and start again on the same sheet of paper, maybe leaving the vestiges of the previous attempt to show you where you went wrong).

When painting interiors it is essential to determine the light source as this area of the paper will be left white. Work away from the light source to the darkest areas of the picture.

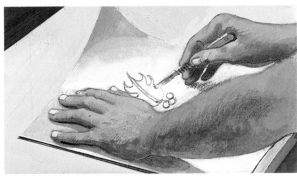

Top: Having first made the design, trace down the image on stout paper or thin card.

Middle: Cut out the design with a sharp pointed knife or a designer's scalpel.

Bottom: Use a stipple brush to dab on paint, which should be thick.

Far right: Finished designs.

Watercolours are usually one-offs, but there may be occasions where you want repeats, perhaps for personalized Christmas cards. There is no way you can repeat a watercolour *exactly*, but you can get a close approximation by using homemade stencils. It is easy to make a stencil. The best kind of material is fairly thick polythene of the type used to make office folders or envelopes. Trace the subject with tracing-paper, and then place carbon paper between the tracing-paper and the polythene. You then go over the tracing with a ball-point pen or a hard pencil of at least 2H grade. Do not use subjects with interior spaces, as these pieces will drop out when you cut out your stencil. You can use either the cut-out part, or the empty space from which the cut-out comes.

To cut out the stencil you need a pair of small scissors or a scalpel (available from good art shops, and more suitable than craft knives as they are smaller). You can prepare the paper with a wash if you wish, wait for it to dry *thoroughly*, and then, firmly holding the stencil down on the paper, go *over* the polythene with your second wash so that the paint outlines

your subject. This is when you are using the actual cut-out. If you are using the polythene from which the cut-out has been extracted, you will lay your wash over the space and over the adjacent area of stencil. Take care in lifting the stencil up, preferably leaving it there until the wash has dried. You should find that you have your design just as you traced it in.

There are many different ways you can use stencils. You can overlap the washes, you can add pure colour to the wash design, and, by not applying a first all-over wash, you can draw the subject in masking fluid. If you do this you can take off the stencil when the fluid has dried (not long) and apply an all-over wash to the paper. When this wash has thoroughly dried, you can peel off the masking fluid, and thus you have a white design to which you can do what you like. A smooth paper is preferable to rough when using stencils.

Stencils can be very intricate, and it is well worth spending time on the cutting-out process. If you enjoy experimenting, the use of stencils can be very stimulating. Overlapping stencils can create new shapes to fire the imagination.

77

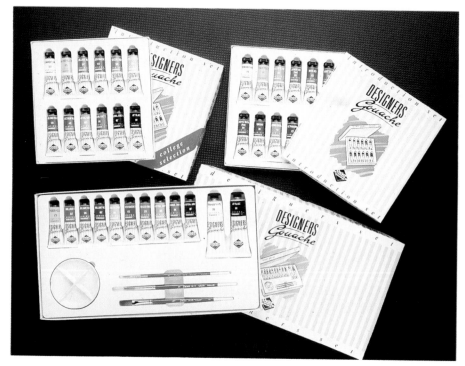

GOUACHE

It is not a difficult transition from orthodox watercolour to gouache, and you can use the same equipment, plus bristle brushes and a palette knife. There is no need to change brushes if you are employing both gouache and watercolour in the same picture, and indeed gouache diluted is not far removed from ordinary watercolour, though perhaps a little grainier. You can therefore lay a wash in gouache exactly as you would do with watercolour. Indeed, almost everything that has been written about watercolour applies to gouache. Gouache lends itself to large designs, so larger brushes, including household decorating brushes, can be employed. You can use gouache by itself, or in association with any of the water-based mediums. It is perfect for fine and 'hard line' work, though if it is used thickly there *is* a tendency for subsequent detail to 'float' on top.

Gouache dries lighter than when first applied, but this affects mainly the pastel tints, and the blacks and dark colours are very solid when used at full strength. The caps of gouache tubes should always be kept on otherwise the paint will dry out; it dries out far more rapidly than the pigment in watercolour tubes. An absolutely solid tube of paint can be annoying, but it *can* be used by scraping out the paint and putting it in the depressions of a palette. You will never be able to recapture the full density of the stronger colours, but it will remain workable.

Watercolour paper takes gouache very well indeed, but mounting board and card are also excellent surfaces, as gouache does not need a tooth and if a smooth effect is wanted there is no better medium. Gouache in pans is not nearly so pleasant to use. Gouache is *not* such a powerful covering agent as acrylic, and for quick successive thick coats of paint acrylic is better. If you are using a thick creamy mix of gouache always start with enough, because its tendency to dry out lighter makes it very difficult to repeat the exact colour when mixing up a fresh quantity. For an all-over, absolutely even, matt surface, gouache is supreme, and it is ideal for decorative purposes, having the virtues of tempera. Gouache is a refined form of distemper, and for very large areas some artists use distemper and its various modern offshoots.

Tempera, which has only quite recently been commercially packaged, is a delightful medium, and most of what has been written about watercolour and gouache apply to it. Tempera dries more rapidly and is more delicate without quite the covering capacity of gouache and is best

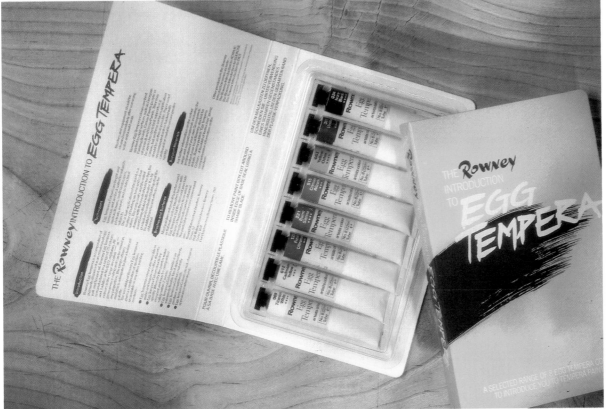

The *Adoration* (above), a painting by Botticelli, who used the method called tempera in which the pigment is ground with egg yolk to give an adhesive and binding quality to the paint. The artists of the Renaissance built up their paintings with a succession of wash glazes. *The Adoration* is one of the finest examples of the use of tempera.

Far left: A selection of gouaches and tempera which can be bought commercially in pots or tubes.

applied in strokes.

As a preliminary exercise, the sea scene mentioned is an ideal starting-off point. Put in all the components firmly in pencil, and fill in the areas with flat colour, ignoring light and shade, and making a pattern of the subject. You can use a large flat soft brush of sable or nylon for the larger areas, a smaller flat one for the boat and the land, and make certain that there is no overlap of colour by drawing the brush sideways along the outlines. If there is a mast on the ship this can be put in with a small sable. To get a really crisp horizon, lay a strip of masking tape along the horizon line and apply the paint so that it overlaps the tape. If you do a still-life study in gouache you can begin by laying a wash of much diluted gouache over the entire paper surface, rough in your design (better at this stage as diluted gouache is a better covering agent than watercolour), and build up, gradually reducing the amount of water in your mix so that at the end you are using the gouache straight from the tube. Do not leave paper peeping through for your highlights, but use white paint.

Watercolour and gouache can be mixed together, and so of course can other mediums, such as pastel and ink, in fact anything which is compatible with water. If things go impossibly wrong but there is a skeleton there somewhere which is worth working on, use a sponge and take off the top surface, or even soak the painting under a tap. If you have provided a pencil drawing as a basis this will eventually reveal itself, and if you have used pen-and-ink on top of gouache, when the gouache is removed the pen-and-ink will also disappear.

In this picture the artist has used a variety of mediums – gouache, pen-and-ink and pastel.

Gouache is an ideal medium for applying areas of flat colour such as in the background of this street scene. Pen-and-ink work has then been added to give the painting an 'illustrative' effect.

82

Gouache and watercolour as washes can be successfully combined with pen and waterproof ink to add colour and depth to a drawing.

Winter scenes containing snow can be something of a challenge, and it often helps to counteract the sheer intense white of the snow with off-white.

Far right: An impressionistic watercolour study. There were seven stages in its genesis:
(1) a charcoal sketch;
(2) a wash of Payne's grey and ultramarine for the sky, the clouds being taken out with blotting paper; (3) the first shadows were added to the land-based objects, in Payne's grey and raw umber; (4) the sea was put in with washes of viridian with blue and raw umber, much diluted, blending in with an orange wash which became the sandy foreground. Payne's grey was added at the foot of the picture. The orange and grey washes were allowed to overlap the shadows; (5) the local colour was put in with crimson, burnt sienna, and yellow ochre, and some detail was added; (6) the shadows were reinforced, and the horizon was affirmed with ultramarine; (7) the picture was tidied up (but not too much so) and the outlines of the objects were strengthened with vandyke brown. Foreground detail was applied in burnt sienna, yellow ochre, and Payne's grey. Throughout the painting process, no colour was used at anything like full strength. The paper used was a heavyweight watercolour paper, slightly rough and therefore was a discouragement to pettifogging detail. Two soft brushes were used, a half-inch flat, and a medium (number three) pointed.

Right: A wartime 'home front' scene carried out in a series of self-contained flat washes in a colour scheme restricted to browns and greens. There was no improvisation in this watercolour and the whole was laid down in pencil, with the exception of the sky. The white everywhere is the white of the paper showing through, and some of the textures are produced by rubbing off the wash with an eraser, which gives a pleasant mottled effect (useful also for mist effects).

86

Watercolour washes are
perfect for sketching animals
and pets.

Facing page, top: The projection of slides onto a wall or canvas is another method used by artists to enlarge photographs.

Facing page, right: In the Middle Ages, the camera lucida was used to project images.

Facing page, left: A pantograph is an excellent instrument for enlarging (or reducing) an original on to paper. The size is varied simply by changing the radius of the pencil arm.

Below: Drawing a grid on any print or photograph is an excellent method of enlarging it accurately.

SHORT CUTS

Someone who is very good at painting can be hopeless at drawing, but there are a number of short cuts. You can trace your design, and get it down onto the paper by using black carbon paper and a sharp-pointed pencil. You can use a slide projector to project transparencies onto a sheet of paper fixed to a screen and then paint the image. With watercolour the brush has to be kept moist rather than loaded, otherwise the paint will drip down the paper; the same applies if an episcope is used. This problem does not arise with gouache, tempera, or pen-and-ink. If you are using pen-and-ink try to hold the pen slightly downwards so that the ink runs down the nib and not up it and onto the pen-holder and the fingers.

An episcope is a box-like device with a lens similar to that of a camera (which is pushed in and out depending on the size of the image wanted), a bright interior light, and a system of mirrors. An illustration of any kind, black-and-white or coloured, is placed on a kind of window and the image is reflected onto a screen.

Then there is freehand copying, and part-freehand copying where the main features but not the detail can be put in by tracing and carbon paper. Many professional artists use, for reference, portfolios of photographs and illustrations cut from newspapers, magazines, periodicals and books, and these are not only useful to jog the memory but can also spark off ideas for pictures only remotely concerned with the particular illustration being looked at.

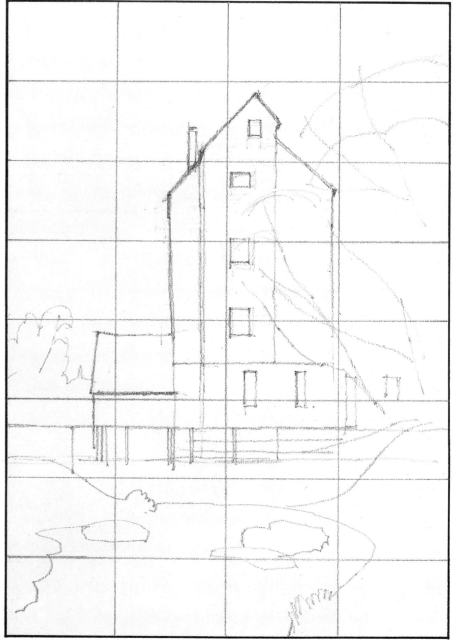

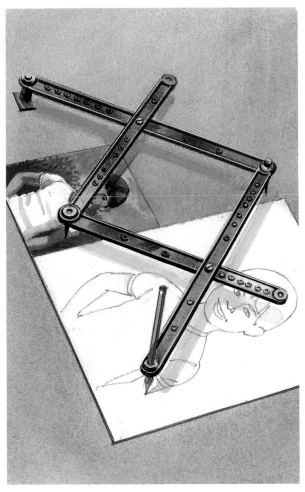

Artillery Officer
by Théodore Géricault.